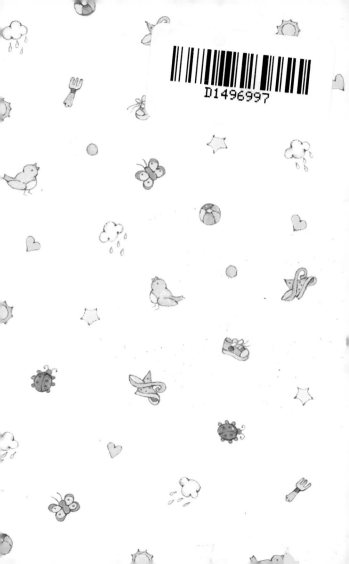

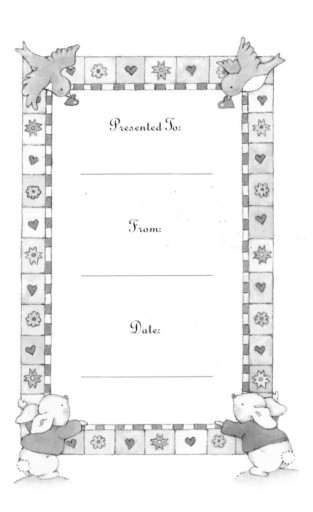

Presented To:

_____

From:

_____

Date:

_____

Baby's First
Book of Prayers

By Melody Carlson
Illustrated By Judith Pfeiffer

CANDLE
BOOKS

Baby's First Book of Prayers
Published by Candle Books 2004
(a publishing imprint of Lion Hudson plc)
Distributed by Marston Book Services Ltd
PO Box 269, Abingdon, Oxon OX14 4YN

Worldwide coedition organised and produced by
Lion Hudson plc, Mayfield House, 256 Banbury Road,
Oxford, OX2 7DH, England.
Tel: +44 (0) 1865 302750 Fax: +44 (0) 1865 302757
Email: coed@lionhudson.com
www.lionhudson.com

ISBN: 1 85985 536 9

Printed in China

Contents

This New Day

Thank you, God, for this great day!

The sun is up, and I must say,

I'm as happy as can be

For each new day you give to me.

Amen

Thank You for My Breakfast

There's a rumble in my tummy,

I smell something that smells yummy!

I see breakfast. It looks good.

Thank you, God! Please, bless my food.

Amen

Step by Step

I learn something new each day,

Step by step along my way.

Thank you, God, for how I grow,

And thank you for the things I know.

Amen

Bless Me as I Play

I love to laugh! And I love fun!

I can wriggle and I can run,

I can jump and skip all day.

Bless me, God, while I'm at play.

Amen

The Green, Green Grass

Good for rolling and bare toes,

The green, green grass grows and grows!

Thank you, God, for this fine treat,

Soft and cushy 'neath my feet!

Amen

Bless My Home

Bless my home, dear God, I pray,

Keep it safe by night and day.

Bless each room and bless each wall.

Bless my family. Bless us all!

Amen

I Am Getting Bigger

When I stretch my hands up high,

I can almost reach the sky.

I am growing tall and straight.

Thank you, God! You're really great!

Amen

Bless Mummy

She shows me how to tie my shoe,

And gives good hugs and kisses too.

She cares for me, and all the rest.

God bless Mummy, she's the best!

Amen

Thank You for the Sun

The sunlight shines across my bed.

It wakes me up. It warms my head.

It makes my world a lot more fun.

Thank you, God, for your bright sun!

Amen

Thank You for My Nose

Thank you, God, for eyes that see

And ears that listen carefully.

Thank you, God, for my smart nose,

It knows a pickle from a rose.

Amen

Fingers and Toes

Fingers do so many things–

Pick up pennies and wear rings.

God made toes to help us stand,

And to wiggle in the sand.

Amen

Thank You for Laughter

Giggles gurgle in my tummy

Each time I see something funny.

Laughing is more fun than toys.

Thank you, God, for happy joys!

Amen

Help Me to Share

Even though I try to mind,

I'm not always very kind.

I know it's right to give and care.

Help me, God. Teach me to share.

Amen

Thank You for Flowers

Thank you, God, for birds and bees.

Thank you, God, for cherry trees.

Thank you, God, for springtime showers.

Thank you, God, for pretty flowers.

Amen

Bless My Friends

I visit friends so we can play.

I wish that I could stay all day.

I like my friends, both short and tall.

God, bless my friends.

Please bless them all!

Amen

I'm Sorry, God

Sometimes I do something bad,

And it makes you very sad.

I'm as sorry as can be.

Thank you for forgiving me.

Amen

On the Go

I like wheels and things that go–

Zipping fast or cruising slow.

In a rocket, or a sleigh,

God, bless us as we go our way!

Amen

Thank You for My Lunch

It always happens, every day,

I eat something, then I play.

Today it's soup, I have a hunch.

Thank you, God, I like my lunch!

Amen

Thank You for the Rain

Huge clouds, like pillows, fill the sky,

Full of tears, they weep and cry.

And even though it seems a pain,

I thank you, God, for sending rain.

Amen

Help Me to Be Kind

Please, help me to do what I should,

To love and share and to be good,

To care for others and be kinder,

I may need a good reminder.

Amen

Wiggles and Giggles

Thank you, God, for toes that wiggle

And ticklish tummies that can giggle.

Thank you, God, for silly things

Like clowns and jokes and slinky springs!

Amen

When I Am Sad

Sometimes when my heart feels bad,

And I'm feeling very sad,

Even if I shed a tear,

I still know that God is here.

Amen

Thank You for My Toys

Thank you, God, for stuff that's fun,

Balls and blocks and things that run.

When I'm done each day with play,

I'll thank you for this happy day.

Amen

Thank You for Rest Time

I love to hop and jump and go,

I never want the fun to slow.

But I guess you know what's best,

Thank you, God, for giving rest.

Amen

Bless Daddy

I love when Daddy carries me,

Like I'm flying fast and free,

Or when we dance a funny jig.

Bless my Daddy. Bless him big!

Amen

Thanks for Hugs

Some hugs are squishy, stiff, or strong.

Some are short and some are long.

Some are cosy, warm, and snug.

Thank you, God, for making hugs!

Amen

My Happy Heart

Sometimes I want to sing and shout.

I want to let my feelings out.

Thank you, God, for loving me—

And now I'll sing so happily!

Amen

Funny Faces

I can wink or grin or frown,

Or be funny, like a clown.

Thank you, God, for this great face.

'Cause I can take it everyplace!

Amen

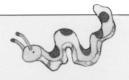

Creepy Crawlies

Thank you, God, for bugs that crawl.

Some are long and some are small.

Some have wings and some are hairy.

Some are big and sort of scary.

Amen

Thank You for Smiles

Thank you, God, for happy smiles.

Some can last for miles and miles.

It's good to take a smile with you

To share with someone who feels blue.

Amen

In Your Big Hands

The world is big. I know it's true.

But, God, it's not too big for you.

In your big hands, we all can rest

You keep us safe. You do what's best.

Amen

The Birds That Sing

I love to hear the robins sing,

and other birds twittering.

They sail around the sky of blue

And chirp to God, "How we love you!"

Amen

Blowing a Kiss

Sometimes it looks like I'm alone,

But, God, you're right here too.

I tell you just how great you are,

And blow a kiss to you!

Amen

Thank You for My Dinner

Thank you, God, for food to eat.

It tastes so good. Oh, what a treat!

Bless our meal, dear God, I pray,

And thank you for this special day.

Amen

Handy Hands

Hands come in handy

For finger painting and hugging Mandy.

And for counting—fingers go to ten.

Thank you, God, for all of them!

Amen

Watch Over Me

God, I know that you can see

Everything—and you see me!

And even if I have a scare

I know I'm safe within your care.

Amen

Furry Things

Thank you, God, for things with fur,

Things with tails and things that purr.

I love puppies, cats, and mice,

And guinea pigs are really nice!

Amen

When Tears Fall

Things don't always go just right,

Sometimes there's trouble or a fight.

I trust you, God, when teardrops fall,

I know that you can dry them all.

Amen

The Moon and Stars

I thank you, God, for quiet night,

For the silver moon so big and bright.

For the starry sky and each bright spark.

For keeping our world from being dark.

Amen

Thank You for My Bed

At night I am a sleepyhead,

And I am thankful for my bed.

I pray, dear God, you'll send moonbeams,

And give me good and pleasant dreams!

Amen

Good Night, God

Good night, dear God, now I must sleep,

I'll close my eyes and slumber deep.

I know you watch me from above,

And cover me with your sweet love.

Amen

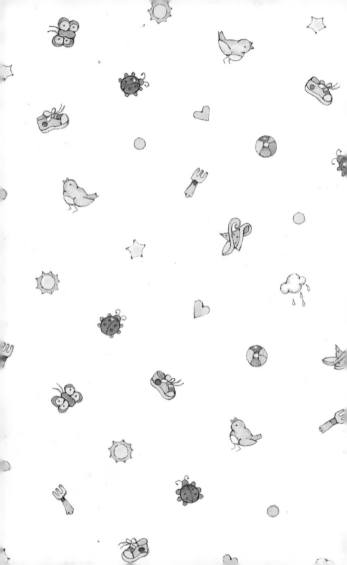